SIMPLY THE BEST
DECORATING RECIPES

MARIAN GETZ

INTRODUCTION BY WOLFGANG PUCK

AS I LEARNED LONG AGO, ALONGSIDE MY MOTHER AND GRANDMOTHER, YOU SHOULD ALWAYS PUT LOTS OF LOVE INTO EVERYTHING YOU COOK. THIS IS CERTAINLY EVIDENT IN THIS COOKBOOK.

Wolfgang Puck

Throughout my career as a chef, I have always held the world of desserts in high regard. Perhaps this is a result of my rather large sweet tooth. It may also be because dessert is the last course of a meal and you want your guests to end their dining experience on a positive note. We tend to eat with our eyes first and a well decorated dessert is one of the best ways to make a great impression on your friends and family. With the help of my new decorating set and this cookbook, anybody can learn to create beautiful cakes and desserts.

Marian was thrilled to write a cookbook to accompany the decorating set. Her years of experience as a district trainer for cake decorators as well as being the executive pastry chef at one of my busiest restaurants more than qualifies her to author this cookbook. She has provided easy to follow step-by-step photo instructions for many of the recipes and has included helpful tips throughout this cookbook.

A student of cooking and baking is probably one of the best ways to describe Marian. She is always looking for something new, something fresh, something local, something seasonal. Her culinary knowledge combined with her passion for cooking and baking is second to none. The recipes that Marian has written for this cookbook will help, inspire and encourage you.

TABLE OF CONTENTS

HELPFUL TIPS

Many recipes in this book require a finished baked cake that is then decorated according to the recipe. In order to bake the cakes before decorating, first choose a flavor of cake you like from pages 78-83, next choose a filling from pages 100-102 (or use buttercream instead) and finally a suitable frosting from pages 90-98 (because it dries very hard, royal icing is for messages and accent pieces only). Cake and filling flavor are personal choices so we give you many options. Once the cake is ready, you can then start the fun by experimenting with the decorating set and the step-by-step photo instructions in this book.

Baking Tips

Baking is often thought of as a difficult task requiring a lot of knowledge and skill. The truth is that anyone can bake if you know these five main things to ensure baking success every time:

- Measure accurately every time.

- Use good equipment, even if it is basic.

- Know your oven well, if its temperature is accurately calibrated and use an oven thermometer.

- Use baking nonstick spray, not butter or regular nonstick spray. It is specifically made so that it ensures that your cake will release from the pan in pristine shape. Use it generously, covering all parts of the interior of the pan right before you are going to pour the batter into it.

- Use a timer, the kind that can travel with you from room to room such as your phone or smart watch.

Be Organized

Be organized and read through the recipe once completely. Gather all the ingredients together before you start to measure or mix anything.

Accurate Measuring

Accurate measuring is critical to achieving success in baking. Use glass measuring cups with measurement markings for liquid ingredients and metal measuring cups for dry ingredients. The measuring spoons I prefer are long and narrow so they will fit in the neck of a spice jar.

Measuring in Piles

I recommend measuring in piles to keep track of ingredients. For example, in a mixing bowl, add the flour, then a separate pile of sugar, a separate pile of baking powder etc. Drop those ingredients into separate little piles but close together then repeat with the rest of the ingredients. This allows you to review the ingredients you have already used and keep track of what needs to be added. If you mix all the ingredients together, you will be more likely to forget ingredients which will result in an undesired outcome and may discourage you from baking in the future.

Baking

Use baking nonstick spray generously then fill your baking vessel such as a baking pan, metal mixing bowl or cupcake mold no more than 2/3 full of batter. Bake cakes in the center of the oven, rotating them halfway through the baking cycle, and place an empty rack above the cake if possible. You can place an empty sheet pan on the empty rack if your cake darkens too fast as it will deflect much of the heat and reduce overbrowning.

Prevent Sticking

To prevent baked goods from sticking, use parchment paper, baking nonstick spray, or nonstick aluminum foil (which is coated with silicone for easy release).

Baking Temperature and Time Guidelines

The baking temperature and baking times listed in the recipes are suggestions rather than exact numbers. Many factors influence the baking times such as the quality of the ingredients and the calibration and quality of your oven. In addition, the size of the pan used also affects how long something needs to be baked. For example, a cupcake bakes in far less time than a large cake. One of the most frequently asked questions in the culinary world is how to tell when food is done? The best way to test most baked goods such as cakes and cupcakes for doneness is to insert a wooden pick or bamboo skewer off-center. When removed, it should generally come out with just a few moist crumbs clinging to it. A streak of shiny batter on the wooden pick indicates that additional baking time is needed. You can also test doneness using a thermometer. Your cakes and cupcakes are done when the internal temperature measured at the center registers 200°F on the thermometer. For brownies and cookies, the top should be dry and a knife inserted in the center should come out clean. Cheesecakes are done when they jiggle but not ripple or when internal temperature at the center measures 155°F using a thermometer.

Leveling Cakes

If your cake emerges from the oven with a peak or hump in the middle, wait until cool then use a serrated knife to cut off all parts of the hump until cake is level. A leveled cake makes for a more professional looking cake, especially once frosted.

Cake Layers

Many of the cakes in this book are tall and cannot be baked in one piece. This means you will need to bake two or more layers of cake to achieve the desired height. In addition, once cakes are cooled and before you begin decorating, you will fill (if desired), stack then frost the cake. See how to fill, stack and frost a cake on page 8 for more instructions.

Do not split cake layers as it creates a large amount of loose crumbs and makes the layers less stable. When you don't split layers, you won't need a crumb coat of frosting in addition to a final coat, making it much faster to frost the cake in one step.

Filling Cake Layers

A filling is put between cake layers to add flavor to a cake and act as "glue" between cake layers to give the cake more stability. There are several filling options to choose from on page 100 to 102 depending on your taste. To add filling, follow the steps on page 8 by first piping a frosting "dam" to keep the filling in place then adding the filling to the center. Make sure the filling is not higher than the "dam". If you do not want to add a filling, simply spread the top of the cake layer(s) with buttercream which will also act as "glue" to keep the cake stable.

Butter

All of the butter used in this book is unsalted. Cool butter is butter that has been left at room temperature for about 30 minutes until it is cool and waxy when pressed with your thumb. It shouldn't be rock hard and it should not be shiny or soft to the touch. This is the best temperature for making buttercream. Use very thinly sliced butter (about 1/8-inch thin) when making buttercream and adding it to the mixer. Softened butter means butter that has been left at room temperature for several hours. It should be soft enough to offer no resistance whatsoever when sliced with a knife. While there is no substitute for the pure flavor of butter, you can use a butter alternative such as vegan margarine or coconut oil and most of the recipes will turn out fairly well.

Sugar Substitute

If you need to use a sugar substitute, choose the one you like best. Cakes will turn out fairly okay but frostings are more difficult. Sugar-free cake mixes turn out reliably.

DECORATING TIPS

Let Cool

Your baked goods such as cakes or cupcakes need to be completely cool before decorating. Never try to frost a cake that is still warm or the buttercream will melt. I prefer to decorate a frozen cake so I bake cakes a minimum of one day before putting them in the freezer. Frozen or chilled cakes are firmer and have much less loose crumbs that get pulled into the frosting while decorating.

Frosting Consistency

Your frosting must be the right consistency. If the frosting is too soft or wet it will slide off the cake and any piping will sag. The rapid tips will not work at all if the frosting is too soft. If it is too firm, it will not spread on the cake well and cause crumbs to be pulled into the icing which ruins the cake's appearance. Heavy, cold or dry buttercream does not pipe well from a pastry bag and will make your hand sore from having to apply a lot of pressure. Buttercream is right when it is at a cool room temperature, is fluffy, light, smooth and holds its shape very well. If you are struggling with cake decorating, chances are that your frosting is either too soft or too firm.

Squeeze and Pull

"Squeeze and pull" is the thing you need to remember when piping anything. Think of squeezing the piping bag (applying pressure) as squeezing toothpaste out of a tube. When you "squeeze", frosting comes out of the tip and when you "pull" the bag along, frosting follows wherever you move your hand. Your dominant hand should be used to squeeze low on the piping bag close to the tip for better control while the other hand is used as support under the other wrist and the bulky part of the piping bag. Practice on parchment until you get the hang of it. You can always scrape up the buttercream and use it again until you are confident.

Store-Bought Cake Mixes & Canned Frosting

It is a shame that we have such great cake mixes yet somewhat less great frostings available at our grocery stores. The images on the box are so misleading as we tend to think that we need a single box of cake mix and a single can of frosting to make the cake pictured on the box. In reality, you would actually need two cake mixes and at least three cans of frosting. While a lot of frosting gets scraped off, a large amount of frosting to start with is necessary to properly frost a cake. In addition, the canned frostings, especially the ones that are not chocolate, are far too soft to adhere well to the sides of a cake or for piping. I think this is why so many of us bake a cake in a 9x13-inch pan and frost it directly in the pan or just buy a finished cake.

Cake Turntable and Icer Tip

A cake turntable, also known as rotary cake stand or revolving cake decorating stand will make your cake decorating experience much better and easier. It lets your flow of frosting pipe easily and more smoothly. It also helps you access all sides of your cake effortlessly. You can start with an inexpensive plastic turntable but the best ones have heavy cast iron bases and aluminum tops. They are best fitted with a silicone, nonslip mat with measure markings so you can center your cake at a glance. A centered cake makes applying the frosting much easier.

An icer tip is an extra large tip that goes inside a large piping bag. It is used to pipe large swaths of frosting to the top and sides of a cake in exactly the right thickness. This makes it easy to get the frosting all over the exposed parts of the cake and greatly reduces the likelihood of pulling cake crumbs into the frosting. After using the icer tip, use a spatula to smooth the sides and top then use a side scraper to make sure the sides are straight and smooth. Finish by smoothing the top from the outside inward towards the center top of the cake using a spatula.

Food Coloring

You can use gel, paste or even the dry, powdered food coloring for decorating. I prefer gel food coloring available in small bottles with twist open/close lids. The food coloring available in little pots is messy to use but far superior to the small tear-drop shaped food coloring available in a boxed set of four. If you are trying to avoid dyes and colors, try using all natural food coloring available at health food stores and online. All natural food coloring tend to be more subtle, muted and much softer than traditional food coloring. I happen to like this look and enjoy using them when making treats for my grandkids.

Additional Piping Bags and Tips

Most cake projects will require several piping bags and multiple tips. To make it easier and more efficient, use additional, purchased piping bags made from either silicone, canvas or plastic. Do not assume that you should be using small bags. A piping bag is never filled more than 2/3 full so if you are holding a 16-inch piping bag you will only be using 12 inches of it. The rest is used for twisting the bag closed. An overfilled bag is very hard to control and the piped creation tends to look wobbly. For small amounts of frosting, I really like to use a piping bag made from parchment paper. You can also use a plastic zipper top bag although it is my least favorite as the rectangular shape is unnaturally wide as you hold it and the pointed end is wide as well which somewhat obstructs your view as you pipe.

Piping a Message on a Cake

Piping a message on a cake can be scary when you are first starting out. If you make a mistake or pipe a crooked or wobbly letter, it is very difficult to remove it from the top of the cake as the frosting under it is so soft. It is a good idea to test piping a message on a piece of parchment paper before doing it on the cake directly. If you want to avoid this problem altogether, you can use the royal icing on page 99 as it dries very hard. Just pipe the message on parchment paper making sure the words are connected and have a "stem" such as a bamboo skewer embedded in part of the icing before drying. Once it has dried uncovered for 24 hours at room temperature, simply peel off the now hardened message and stand it up on the cake. The height that the message creates adds to the overall height of the cake which makes it look even more impressive. You can see an example of this in the baby shower cake recipe on page 32.

How to Fill, Stack and Frost a Cake

Before you begin decorating, fill your cake if desired then stack and frost as needed. Below are the steps on how to fill, stack and frost a cake. If you are not using filling, you can simply use buttercream between the cake layers.

DECORATING TIPS

1 Place cake on a cardboard cake round. Pipe a "dam" of frosting around the perimeter using the large round tip. This "dam" of solid frosting will keep the softer filling in place.

2 Add the softer filling to the center of the cake. Ensure it is lower in height than the frosting "dam".

3 Add the top layer of cake and gently press into place. This is called "stacking".

4 To begin frosting the cake, add a generous pile of frosting to the top.

5 Glide spatula over frosting to spread. Don't pull spatula straight up as it will pull frosting from the cake resulting in cake crumbs mixing into the frosting.

6 "Mushroom" frosting over cake top edge evenly. This will help connect frosting put on side of cake later.

7 Smooth out top frosting, leaving overhanging frosting in place.

8 Hold spatula vertical and straight to frost sides. Glide back and forth without pulling spatula away from the cake.

9 Once cake is covered, check that cake is reasonably level, vertically straight without any large holes or divots.

Use a cake side scraper held vertically and straight, touching the base of the turntable. Glide around cake as your other hand turns the turntable. Repeat until smooth and even. Clean scraper after each turn by scraping it on the lip of the mixing bowl containing the frosting.

Clean off scraper after each pass or you will end up wiping the frosting back on the cake which will prevent it from looking smooth.

Use edge of scraper to remove excess frosting from cake base.

Use the spatula to smooth the top, removing some frosting with each pass. Start at the outer edge, glide to the cake center then glide off. Clean spatula after every pass until smooth. A cake is never perfect. Aim for a nice finish instead.

Finished cake ready to decorate.

Parchment Bag

If you need additional piping bags, you can make them yourself using parchment paper, disposable plastic bags or plastic zip top bags. Here are instructions how to easily make a parchment piping bag:

Hold your finger on the center long side of a rectangular piece of parchment paper then roll up.

Keep finger gently in place as you continue to roll up the paper.

Keep pulling on the tail end while rolling to keep it from falling apart.

While holding bag towards the bottom, drop in desired tip. No coupler needed.

Using scissors, snip off bag tip to expose piping tip. Don't cut off too much or the tip will fall out.

Three examples of piping bags made from parchment, disposable plastic or zip top bag.

Rainbow Pouch

Using a multi-colored frosting pouch (rainbow in this case) can make your decorations really stand out as the multi-colored frosting flows out neatly, especially using the rapid tips. As an example, see the Unicorn Cupcakes recipe on page 16.

On a sheet of plastic wrap, pipe 6-inch rows so they are touching. Make the total width of rows 4-5 inches wide.

Pipe white buttercream on top then use the plastic wrap to roll the frosting into a sausage-shaped tube.

Roll up grasping the ends. Twist ends of plastic wrap firmly to snug frosting into a bundle.

Using scissors, cut off one end of the bundle.

Drop the bundle cut-end first into the large piping bag fitted with coupler and either rapid or ball tip.

The plastic wrap stays inside the bag while you pipe to keep colors neatly together and piping bag mostly clean.

Striping a Bag

Striping a bag is the technique of preparing your piping bag so that the piped exterior color differs from the interior. An example of this technique was used on the Red Velvet Tulip Cake on page 14.

Use a pastry brush and the darkest frosting you are planning on using.

Brush a thin layer of frosting around the inside of the piping bag.

Add lighter frosting to bag but do not fill more than 2/3 full.

Final piped frosting will be "striped".

DECORATING TIPS

10

How to Pipe a Rose

To pipe a rose, you will need firm buttercream, the rose nail and a piping bag fitted with the coupler and small rose tip. It will take a some practice to get the height and shape you want but you can reuse the buttercream while you practice. If you have very warm hands, swap out the buttercream and let it cool until it firms up again before reusing.

Turn nail and pipe a cone of frosting to act as a support structure for the rose petals.

Pipe a second cone base on top of the first.

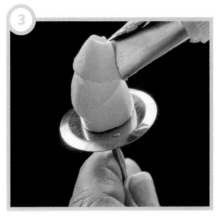

Pipe a third cone. This will be the center of the flower.

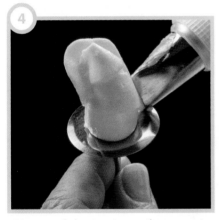

Pipe petals by turning nail as you pipe in an upside-down "U" shape. Start at the base of the nail, pull and pipe up and over then pull and squeeze until you reach the nail base again.

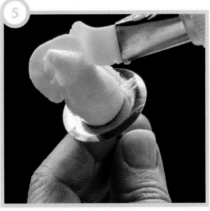

Add 2nd petal starting just behind the last then pipe in the same manner as the 1st petal.

Add the 3rd petal following the directions for the 2nd petal.

The next row of petals repeats exactly like the first three but tip your piping hand slightly outward to help "open up" the petals and make the flower larger.

Add as many petals as you wish or until you can't see the top of the rose nail anymore.

The finished rose. Remove with open scissors and place it on the cake using the scissors to aid you. Close the scissors to get the rose onto the cake.

Piping Tips

Here are some piping examples you can expect from each of the piping tips:

Rapid Tulip Tip

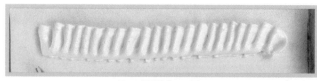

Small Ribbon Tip

Rapid Starburst Tip

Small Zig Zag Tip

Rapid Poppy Tip

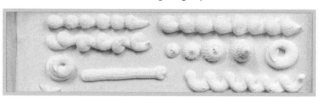

Small Star Tip

Swirl Ball Tip

Small Grass Tip

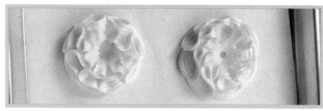

Zig Zag Ball Tip

Small Leaf Tip

Large Round Tip

Small Round Tip

Large Star Tip

Small Rose Tip

PANTRY TIPS

Being prepared to cook or bake the recipes in this book, or any recipe for that matter, is one of the keys to success in the kitchen. Your pantry must be stocked with the basics. We all know how frustrating it can be when you go to the cupboard and what you need is not there. This list includes some of the ingredients you will find in this book and some that I feel are important to always have on hand.

DRY GOODS	REFRIGERATED	FINISHING
Flour or Gluten-Free Flour	Butter	Gumballs
Baking Powder	Eggs	Confetti Sprinkles
Baking Soda	Cream Cheese	Chocolate Jimmies
Salt	Heavy Cream	Coarse Sugar
Sugar	Whole Milk	Nonpareil Sprinkles
Powdered Sugar	Full Fat Buttermilk	Gum Paste
Vanilla	Pasteurized Egg Whites	Fondant
Clear Imitation Vanilla		Candles
Good Quality Cocoa		Ribbons
Good Quality Chocolate		
Gel or Paste Food Colorings		
Shortening		
Vegetable oil		
Corn syrup		

If you are feeling creative, adventurous or just following a recipe, it's great to have a good selection in the kitchen.

RED TULIP CAKE

Note: You will need to fill and stack this cake before decorating

You Will Need:

Red Velvet Cake, see page 82, baked as two 7-inch layers in fluted tart pans and cooled

Choose one of the buttercream frostings, see page 90-92

Choose one of the fillings, see pages 100-102 (or use buttercream instead)

Gel or paste food coloring

Large round tip

Rapid tulip tip

Small leaf tip

1

Using the large round tip and white buttercream, pipe a mound into the center of the cake.

2

Using an off-set spatula, shape the mound into a dome as a base for the flowers.

3

Using the rapid tulip tip with red and white buttercream, pipe flowers around the dome.

4

Pipe additional flowers until dome is covered. Pull center flowers slowly to achieve taller flowers.

5

Using the small leaf tip and green buttercream, pipe leaves between flowers.

UNICORN
CUPCAKES

You Will Need:

Choose a cake flavor, see page 78-83, baked as cupcakes and cooled

Choose one of the buttercream frostings, see page 90-92

Store-bought fondant, see source page 111

Edible gold luster dust, see source page 111

Gel or paste food coloring

Large star tip

Cut out triangles from rolled white and pink fondant.

Place a pink fondant triangle on top of white triangle then score the center as shown.

Pinch together the ends of the triangle opposite to the score then pull off excess, leaving a "stem" to be used to anchor into the buttercream later.

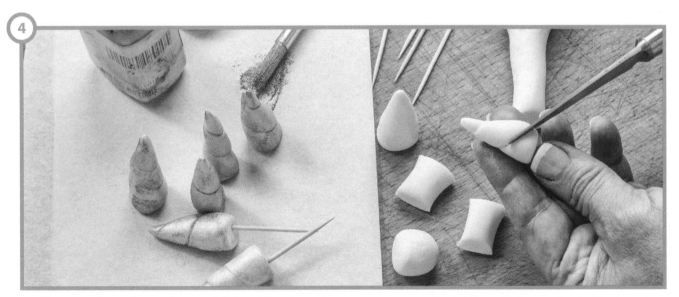

Shape unicorn horns from additional fondant then score around the horns using a paring knife. Insert wooden picks into the horn bottoms then brush each with edible gold dust.

5

Using different colored buttercream, layer rainbow colors on top of each other on top of plastic wrap as shown.

6

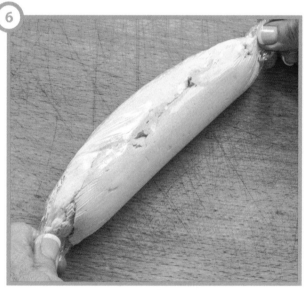

Press plastic wrap around buttercream stack into a sausage shape.

7

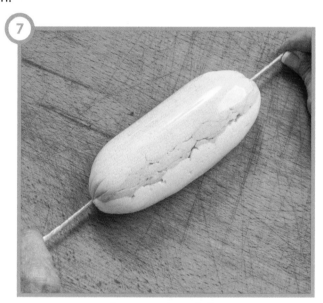

Twist ends tightly.

8

Snip off one end of the bundle using scissors.

9

Attach large star tip to piping bag. Grab bundle by the plastic wrap tail then lower into piping bag with the cut end facing down.

The plastic wrap will stay inside the piping bag and helps keep colors separate and bag clean.

Pipe a large rainbow rosette on top of each cupcake.

Press ears and horn into each cupcake as shown.

SUNFLOWER

Note: You will need to choose a cake batter recipe as well as a buttercream recipe and make two batches of each in order to stack and frost this cake

You Will Need:

Choose a cake flavor, see page 78-83, baked as four 7-inch layers and cooled

Choose one of the buttercream frostings, see page 90-92

Choose one of the fillings, see pages 100-102 (or use buttercream instead)

Chocolate Ganache Frosting, see page 93

Large star tip

Small leaf tip

Small grass tip

1. Using the back of the large star tip, mark cake where you want sunflowers to be piped. This will help you space out the flowers evenly and attractively.

2. Using the small leaf tip and yellow buttercream, pull sunflower petals around each marked circle.

3. Using the small leaf tip and a slightly different yellow buttercream, add accent petals to each flower.

4. Using the small leaf tip and light green buttercream, pipe leaves around sunflowers.

5. Using the small leaf tip and dark green buttercream, pipe additional leaves around sunflowers.

6. Using the small grass tip and ganache, pipe centers into each flower.

ANNIVERSARY CAKE

You Will Need:

Choose a cake flavor, see page 78-83, baked in a 2-quart bowl and cooled

Choose one of the buttercream frostings, see page 90-92

Gel or paste food colorings

Rapid poppy tip

Rapid tulip tip

Small leaf tip

DECORATING

1

Using the rapid poppy and tulip tips as well as various multi-colored buttercream (see striping a bag on page 10), pipe alternating flowers along the bottom of the cake by pressing the tip against the cake, squeezing then pulling away.

2

Create additional rows of flowers around the cake.

3

When you get close to the top, take care with your spacing of the flowers to cover as much of the cake as possible.

4

Towards the top, pull flowers more slowly to achieve taller flowers.

5

Using the small leaf tip and green buttercream, pipe leaves between flowers as desired.

TIP

A cake baked in a bowl is one of the easiest cakes to ice because there aren't layers to deal with. Just be sure to apply baking spray to the bowl, not regular nonstick spray. The rapid tips make covering the cake both easy and flawless. The Wolfgang Puck stainless steel mixing bowls are ideal for making this cake.

CHOCOLATE CHIP
S'MORE CAKE

You Will Need:

One 10-inch Chocolate Chip Cookie Cake, see page 84

Chocolate Ganache Frosting, see page 93

Meringue Frosting, see page 94

A blow torch

Large round tip

Swirl ball tip

Using the large round tip and ganache, pipe a layer of ganache on top of the cookie cake, leaving a 1 1/2-inch border.

Spread ganache evenly using a small off-set spatula.

Using the swirl ball tip and meringue, pipe large puffs on top of the ganache.

Using the large round tip and meringue, pipe a band around the bottom of the cake.

Using a blow torch, brown the meringue as desired.

TIP

Small blow torches can be found in kitchen specialty stores. Regular sized blow torches can be found at home improvement stores. I prefer the regular size as they brown faster and stay lit even when tipped downward.

CACTUS CAKE

You Will Need:

Master Vanilla Cake, see page 80, baked in a 2-quart mixing bowl and cooled

Best Buttercream Frosting, see page 90

Gel or paste food coloring

Large star tip

Small star tip

Small round tip

Small rose tip

Graham cracker crumbs

DECORATING

1

Using the large star tip and dark green buttercream, pipe cacti on and around cake.
Add a small amount of brown or black food coloring for darker shades of green buttercream.

2

Using the small star tip and light green buttercream, pipe different shape cacti on and around cake.

Using the small star tip and medium green buttercream, pipe additional cacti on or around the cake.

Using the small star tip and green buttercream, pipe long cacti on and around cake.

Using the small rose tip and pink buttercream, pipe cactus flowers as desired.

Using the small round tip and white buttercream, pipe thorns as desired.

7

Using the small round tip and yellow buttercream, pipe additional cacti centers as desired.

DECORATING

Spoon crushed graham cracker crumbs around cake.

LEMON
CHEESECAKE

You Will Need:

Lemon Cheesecake, see page 88

Lemon Curd Filling, see page 100

Royal Icing, see page 99

Chocolate Ganache Frosting, see page 93

Whipped Cream Frosting, see page 98

1 lemon, cut into thin half-moon slices

Small star tip

Small round tip

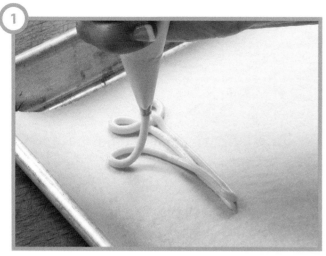

Pipe desired pattern onto parchment paper using the small round tip and yellow royal icing. Let dry uncovered for 24 hours at room temperature. Make extras as they are fragile.

Spread a thin layer of lemon curd over the top of the lemon cheesecake. Leave a 1/4-inch border around the top of the cake.

Using the small star tip and whipped cream, pipe a shell border around the top of the cake.

Press lemon slices around the sides of the cake.

Using the small round tip and ganache, write desired message on top of the cake.

TIP

If you would like to dress this cake up even further, add flowers around the bottom of the cake using the Best Buttercream Frosting on page 90 as well as the rapid tulip or rapid poppy tip. You can also use colored whipped cream instead of ganache to write the message on top of the cake.

BABY SHOWER CAKE

Note: You will need to choose a cake batter recipe as well as a buttercream recipe and make two batches of each in order to fill, stack and frost this cake (see page 8)

You Will Need:

Choose a cake flavor, see page 78-83, baked as two 8-inch and two 4-inch square layers and cooled

Choose one of the buttercream frostings, see page 90-92

Choose one of the fillings, see pages 100-102 (or use buttercream instead)

Royal Icing, see page 99

Gel or paste food colorings

Small round tip

Small rose tip

1 Using the small round tip and yellow royal icing, pipe desired message onto a parchment-lined sheet pan then insert a wooden pick. Let dry uncovered for 24 hours at room temperature. Make extras as they are fragile.

2 Using the small rose tip and pink buttercream, pipe continuous ruffles on top square of the cake. If you find that the top tier of the cake needs extra support to sit on the bottom tier, see step 1 on page 61 on how to add support using a piece of styrofoam and drinking straws.

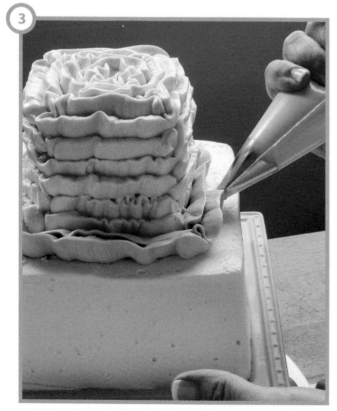

3 Using the small rose tip and blue buttercream, pipe continuous ruffles halfway down the bottom square of the cake.

4 Using the small rose tip and yellow buttercream, pipe remaining bottom square with ruffles. Carefully peel piped message from parchment paper and place on top of cake.

EASTER CHICKS & EGGS

You Will Need:

Deviled eggs, see page 104

Gel or paste food colorings

Thin carrot slices

Whole peppercorns

Lettuce

Small star tip

Small round tip

Color water by adding a few drops of food coloring then place egg whites into water. Keep egg halves in colored water for at least 1 hour before filling so they have time to absorb the color. Thinly julienne lettuce to look like easter grass and arrange on a platter. This will help keep eggs stay in place.

For chicks, cut egg top off while holding egg vertically. For traditional deviled eggs, cut them horizontally. Use small star tip to fill eggs.

For the feet, cut triangles from thin carrot slices then punch out toes using the small round tip. Cut tiny carrot triangles for the beaks and use whole peppercorns for the eyes.

HALLOWEEN CAKE

You Will Need:

Choose a cake flavor, see page 78-83, baked as three 6-inch layers, baked and cooled

Choose one of the buttercream frostings, see page 90-92

Meringue Frosting, see page 94

Chocolate Ganache Frosting, see page 93

Gel or paste food coloring

Large round tip

Small round tip

DECORATING

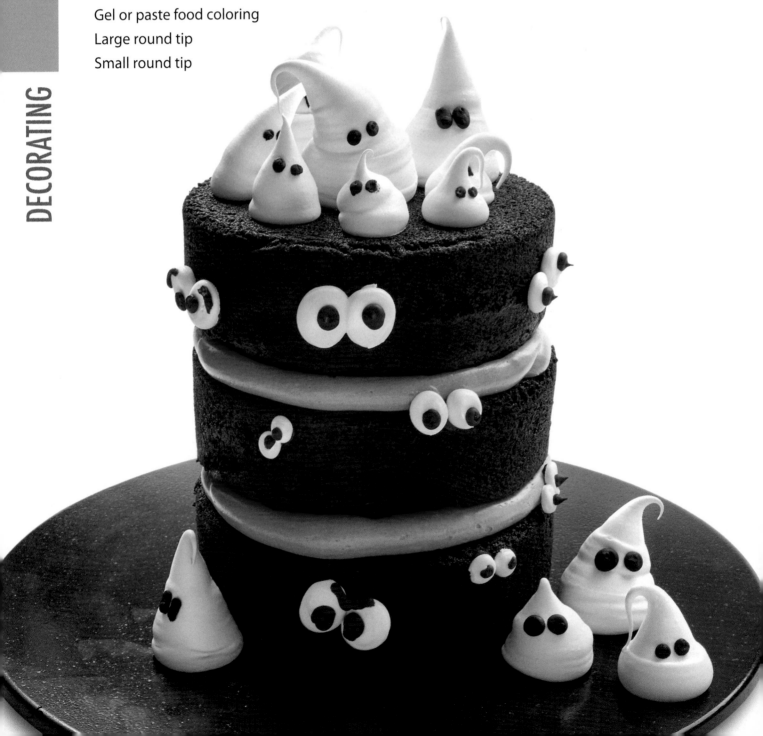

Using the large round tip and meringue, pipe ghosts onto a parchment-lined sheet pan. Using the small round tip, pipe some of the white eye balls and use black colored meringue for the eyes. Let dry uncovered for 24 hours at room temperature.

Place cake into the center of the service tray, making sure it is free of crumbs as the sides will remain exposed.

Using the large round tip and orange buttercream, pipe a band around cake to act as a "dam" for the ganache filling.

Spread ganache into the center of the cake. Repeat to make two additional tiers.

Place ghosts on top of cake as desired.

Using the small round tip and ganache as glue, adhere eye balls around cake at different angles so they look like they are peeking out of the cake.

37

HANUKKAH CAKE

Note: You will need to fill, stack and frost this cake before decorating (see page 8)

You Will Need:

Choose a cake flavor, see page 78-83, baked as two 7-inch layers and cooled

Choose one of the buttercream frostings, see page 90-92

Choose one of the fillings, see pages 100-102 (or use buttercream instead)

Large pretzel rods

White chocolate, melted

Royal Icing, see page 99

Colored sugar and sprinkles

Gel or paste food coloring

Small round tip

Swirl ball tip

1 Dip pretzel rods into melted white chocolate then dip in colored sugar or sprinkles.

2 Using the small round tip and blue royal icing, pipe two triangles to form the Star of David onto a parchment-lined sheet pan then insert a wooden pick. Let dry uncovered for 24 hours at room temperature. Pipe extras as they are fragile.

3 Arrange dipped pretzel rods around the sides of the cake in an alternating fashion.

4 Using the swirl ball tip and white buttercream, pipe large puffs on top of the cake then insert the Star of David into the center. Top with sprinkles.

FOURTH OF JULY
CUPCAKES

You Will Need:

Choose a cake flavor, see page 78-83, baked as cupcakes and cooled

Choose one of the buttercream frostings, see page 90-92

Gel or paste type food coloring

Small grass tip

TIP

You can use the same frosting technique using the colors of your favorite sports team or school. For a cheerleader look, chill the buttercream a bit then pipe the strands taller to look like pom-poms.

DECORATING

1 Apply a thin layer of white buttercream on top of the cupcakes.

2 Using the small grass tip and blue buttercream, pull a starburst pattern around each cupcake.

3 Using the small grass tip and white buttercream, add additional starburst patterns in the center of the cupcake tops.

4 Using the small grass tip and red buttercream, pipe centers of cupcakes.

EASY BIRTHDAY CAKE

Note: You will need to fill, stack and frost this cake before decorating (see page 8)

You Will Need:

Choose a cake flavor, see page 78-83, baked as two 7-inch layers and cooled

Choose one of the buttercream frostings, see page 90-92

Choose one of the fillings, see pages 100-102 (or use buttercream instead)

Gumballs

Candles

Candy sprinkles

Gel or paste food coloring

Large round tip

Zig zag ball tip

Small star tip

1 Using the large round tip and white buttercream, pipe a band around the bottom of the cake. Piping a straight band around the cake is the easiest border to pipe and will help hold gumballs in place.

2 Press gumballs into the piped band around the cake.

3 Using the small star tip and white buttercream, pipe a shell border around the top of the cake.

4 Using the zig zag ball tip and white buttercream, pipe a large puff into the center of the cake.

5 Top cake with colored sprinkles as desired, place a gumball in the center then stick a candle into the center puff.

TIP

Party stores are the best place to find candies, gumballs and sprinkles in individual colors. These make it easy to customize a cake and make it look professional.

THANKSGIVING PUMPKIN CHEESECAKE

You Will Need:

Pumpkin cheesecake, see tip on page 89

Choose one of the buttercream frostings, see page 90-92

Chocolate Ganache Frosting, see page 93

Store-bought fondant

Gel or paste food colorings

Large star tip

Small grass tip

Small round tip

Small star tip

Small leaf tip

TIP
You can also use brown buttercream instead of ganache to make the border around the bottom of the cake.

DECORATING

44

1. Using the small round tip, make a depression into various size orange balls of fondant.

2. Using the edge of any large tip, press curving indentations around the sides of pumpkins from top to bottom.

3. Shape stems from brown fondant, Insert into pumpkins then place pumpkins onto cake.

4. Using the small round tip and green buttercream, pipe vines around pumpkins then use the small leaf tip to add green leaves along vines.

5. Using the small grass tip and green buttercream, pipe grass around pumpkins and around the edge of the cake top.

6. Using the small star tip and ganache, pipe a shell border around the bottom of the cake.

TEACUP
CUPCAKES

You Will Need:

Choose a cake flavor, see page 78-83, baked as cupcakes, cooled then press into teacups

Best Buttercream Frosting, see page 90 or Whipped Cream Frosting, see page 98

Gel or paste food coloring

Candles

Small rose tip

Small leaf tip

DECORATING

1. Using the small rose tip and white buttercream or whipped cream, pipe a ruffle around the top of the cupcake. Keep the narrow end of the tip pointing up while piping. The narrow end is what creates the ruffle.

2. Using the small rose tip and yellow buttercream, pipe a ruffle along the inside of the white ruffle.

3. Fill center of yellow ruffle with additional white ruffles.

4. Finish center with additional yellow ruffles.

5. Using the small leaf tip and green buttercream, pipe leaves around cupcake as desired.

TIP

Since you are using the same small rose tip for both colors and switching back and forth between white and yellow buttercream, use the piping bag with the white buttercream and use a parchment bag for the yellow buttercream then switch the tip between the two bags.

CHRISTMAS

Note: You will need to fill, stack and frost this cake before decorating (see page 8)

You Will Need:

Choose a cake flavor, see page 78-83, baked as two 7-inch layers and cooled

Choose one of the buttercream frostings, see page 90-92

Choose one of the fillings, see pages 100-102 (or use buttercream instead)

Ribbon

Paste or gel food colorings

Small leaf tip

Small round tip

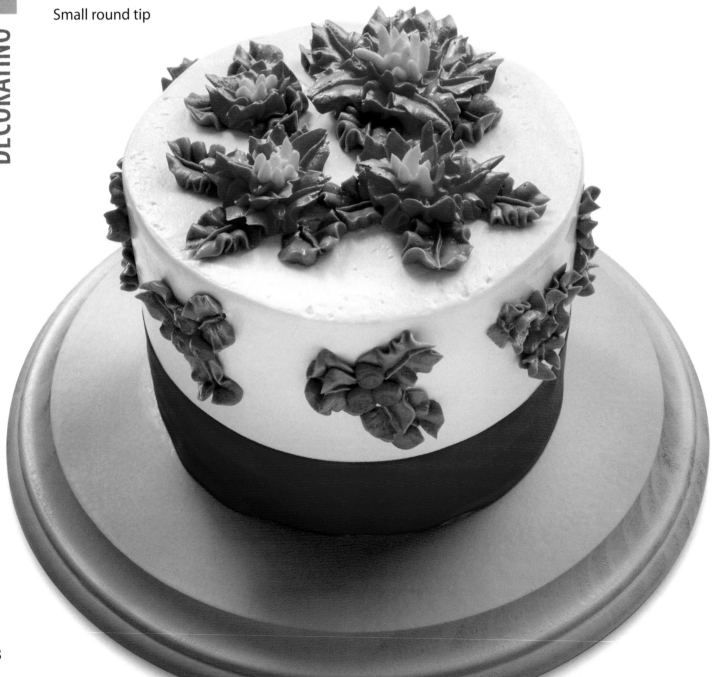

1

Wrap bottom of cake with a red ribbon. It will adhere easily to the buttercream.

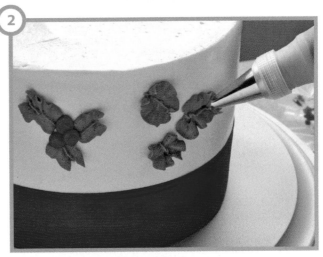

2

Using the small leaf tip and green buttercream, pipe holly leaves in sets of three around the sides of the cake.

3

Using the small round tip and red buttercream, pipe red dots into the center of leaf clusters.

4

Using the small leaf tip as well as red and green buttercream, pipe poinsettias on top of cake.

5

Using the small round tip and yellow buttercream, pipe the centers of the poinsettias.

GRADUATION
HAT

Note: You will need to frost and cover this cake with gum paste before decorating

You Will Need:

Choose a cake flavor, see page 78-83, baked in a 2-quart bowl and cooled

Store-bought gum paste

Choose one of the buttercream frostings, see page 90-92

Gel or paste food colorings

Large round tip

Small grass tip

Small round tip

Small star tip

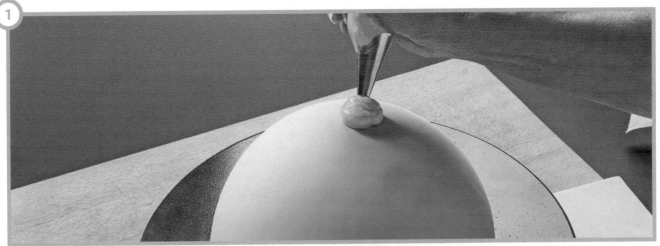

Cover cake in a thin layer of buttercream then cover with gum paste. Roll out a square of gum paste and let air dry for 2 days, flipping over to dry bottom after 1 day. After the 2 days have passed, use the large round tip and yellow buttercream to pipe a mound to act as glue in the center of the graduation hat.

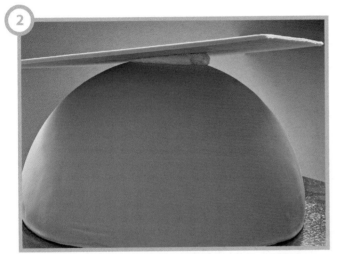

Gently press the mortar board into the yellow buttercream mound and position as desired.

Using the small grass tip and yellow buttercream, pipe the tassel by pulling long strands on top of each other.

Using the small round tip and black buttercream, pipe desired message on top of the hat.

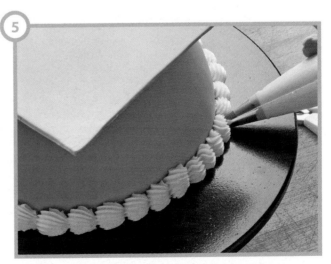

Using the small star tip and white buttercream, pipe a shell border around the base of the graduation hat.

51

FATHER'S DAY
BROWNIE CAKE

Note: You will need to frost this cake before decorating

You Will Need:

Brownie cake, see page 86, baked as a 9x9-inch cake and cooled

Chocolate Ganache Frosting, see page 93

Choose one of the buttercream frostings, see page 90-92

Gel or paste food colorings

Candles

Rapid tulip tip

Small leaf tip

Small star tip

1. Using the rapid tulip tip and multi-colored buttercream, pipe flowers on top of cake, leaving a 1/2-inch border.

2. Using the small leaf tip and green buttercream, pipe leaves between flowers.

3. Using the small star tip and ganache, pipe a shell border around the bottom of the cake.

4. Using the small star tip and ganache, pipe a shell border around the top of the cake.

EASTER BUNNY CUPCAKE

You Will Need:

Choose a cake flavor, see page 78-83, baked as cupcakes and cooled

Store-bought fondant

Coarse sugar

Choose one of the buttercream frostings, see page 90-92

Gel or paste food colorings

Small grass tip

Small rose tip

Small round tip

1 Using white and pink fondant, shape the bunny's body, tail and feet. Dampen bunny tail with a bit of water then roll in coarse sugar. Dampen the area where you will be joining pieces together with just a bit of water. A moist paper towel is the easiest way to do this.

2 Using the small grass tip and green buttercream, pipe grass on top of cupcake.

3 Using the small round tip and yellow buttercream, pipe small flowers in the grass.

4 Using the small round tip and white buttercream, pipe white centers into the flowers.

5 Using the small rose tip and pink buttercream, pipe additional flowers in the grass.

6 Place assembled bunny on top of cupcake.

PRINCESS
CUPCAKES

You Will Need:

Choose a cake flavor, see page 78-83, baked as cupcakes and cooled

Choose one of the buttercream frostings, see page 90-92

Gel or paste food coloring

Small round tip

Small leaf tip

Rapid tulip tip

Using the small round tip and yellow buttercream, pipe edges of cupcakes as shown.

Using the rapid tulip tip as well as pink and white buttercream, pipe flowers on top of cupcakes.

Turn the bag halfway for different color flowers as the white and pink buttercream dispenses differently depending on the bag's angle.

Using the small leaf tip and green buttercream, pipe leaves on top of cupcakes.

CRISPY RICE SQUARES

You Will Need:

Store-bought crispy rice squares

Choose one of the buttercream frostings, see page 90-92

Gel or paste food coloring

Large round tip

Rapid poppy tip

Small leaf tip

1

Using the large round tip and pink buttercream, cover the top of the crispy rice squares.

2

Top each piece with another crispy rice square.

3

Using the rapid poppy tip as well as pink and white buttercream, pipe a flower in the center of each square.

4

Using a small paint brush, gently bend outer flower petals down to open up the flower.

5

Using the small leaf tip and green buttercream, pipe leaves around flowers as desired.

WEDDING
CAKE

Note: You will need to choose a cake batter recipe as well as a buttercream recipe and make two batches of each in order to fill, stack and frost this cake (see page 8)

You Will Need:

Choose a cake flavor, see page 78-83, baked as two 8-inch and two 4-inch cake layers, cooled

Best Buttercream Frosting, see page 90

Choose one of the fillings, see pages 100-102 (or use buttercream instead)

Styrofoam plate, cut into a 4-inch circle

5 plastic drinking straws

Gel or paste food coloring

Small star tip

Small round tip

Small leaf tip

Rapid poppy tip

Place the 4-inch frosted cake tier on the 4-inch styrofoam circle. Press 5 drinking straws straight into the center of the 8-inch frosted cake tier in a circle formation slightly smaller than 4-inches. This will help support the second tier. Use scissors to cut straws flush with the top of the icing so that they are all level. Place the 4-inch tier on top of straw platform. Using the small round tip and yellow buttercream, pipe small dots in groups of three on the side of the cake.

Using the small star tip and light green buttercream, pipe a braided border around bottom of cake.

Using the small star tip and light green buttercream, pipe a shell border around top tier of cake.

Using the small star tip and light green buttercream, pipe a shell border around the top of the cake.

Using the small star tip and light green buttercream, pipe a shell border around the top of the bottom tier of the cake.

Using the small star tip and light green buttercream, pipe a mound into the center of the cake top.

7

Using the rapid poppy tip and pink buttercream, pipe flowers around the mound.

8

Pipe additional pink flowers on top of the bottom tier of the cake as desired.

9

Using the small leaf tip and dark green buttercream, pipe leaves between flowers as desired.

RIBBON
CUPCAKES

You Will Need:

Choose a cake flavor, see page 78-83, baked as cupcakes and cooled

Choose one of the buttercream frostings, see page 90-92

Gel or paste food coloring

Small ribbon tip

Small rose tip

Rose nail

TIP

You can see detailed instructions
on how to pipe a rose on page 11.

Using the small ribbon tip and blue buttercream, pipe a blue ruffle around top of cupcakes. To pipe the ruffle, squeeze the piping bag and turn the cupcake around as you squeeze. The ruffle just happens by itself due to the small ribbon tip.

Using the small rose tip, rose nail and white buttercream, pipe a white rose then place in the center of a cupcake using scissors.

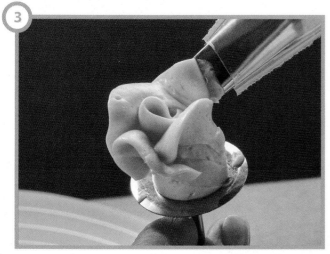

Using the small rose tip, rose nail and pink buttercream, pipe a pink rose.

Place pink rose in center of another cupcake using scissors.

Using the small rose tip, rose nail and yellow buttercream, pipe a yellow rose.

Place yellow rose in center of a third cupcake using scissors.

LAVENDER ROSE CAKE

Note: You will need to fill, stack and frost this cake before decorating (see page 8)

You Will Need:

Choose a cake flavor, see page 78-83, baked as two 7-inch cake layers and cooled

Best Buttercream Frosting, see page 90

Choose one of the fillings, see pages 100-102 (or use buttercream instead)

Gel or paste food coloring

Small star tip

Small round tip

Rose nail

Small rose tip

Small leaf tip

Pick the best looking side of the cake which will be the front of the cake then mark it by using a skewer as shown above. Using the small star tip and lavender buttercream, pipe a reverse shell border around the bottom of the cake. Make sure to start piping in the back of the cake on the opposite side of the skewer so that the piped border meets in the back, leaving the front with a seamless border. Remove skewer once done piping.

Using the small star tip and lavender buttercream, pipe a reverse shell border around the top of the cake.

Using the small rose tip as well as purple and lavender buttercream, pipe a small mound into the center of the cake to make the base for the center rose (see striping a bag on page 10 for how to make multi-colored buttercream).

Using the small rose tip and rose nail, pipe purple and lavender flowers.

Using scissors, place flower on top of the small mound.

Make additional flowers then arrange on top of the cake as desired.

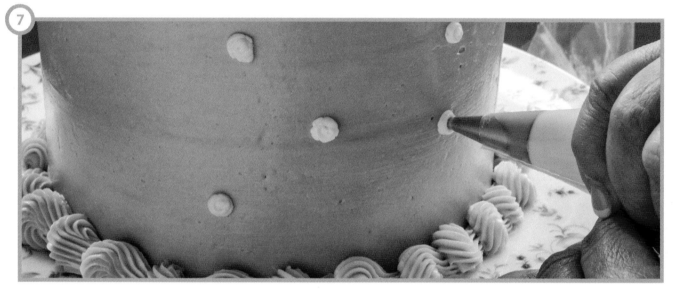

Using the small round tip and white buttercream, pipe small dots in a random pattern around the side of the cake.

Using the small leaf tip and green buttercream, pipe leaves between the roses as desired.

VALENTINE'S
LOVE

Note: You will need to frost this cake before decorating

You Will Need:

Red Velvet Cake, see page 82, baked as an 8-inch heart-shaped layer and cooled

Best Buttercream Frosting, see page 90

Royal Icing, see page 99

Gel or paste food coloring

Small round tip

Large round tip

Rose nail

Small rose tip

Small leaf tip

Using the small round tip and red royal icing, pipe desired message onto a parchment-lined sheet pan. Let dry uncovered at room temperature for 24 hours. Make extras as they are fragile.

Using the small round tip and red buttercream, pipe hearts around the sides of the cake.

Using the large round tip and red buttercream, pipe mounds on top of cake to raise and support roses.

Using the small rose tip and red buttercream, pipe roses using the rose nail.

Lift roses off the rose nail using scissors then place on top of each mound.

Using the small round tip and light green buttercream, pipe rose stems around each rose.

Using the small leaf tip and dark green buttercream, pipe leaves around the roses.

Using the large round tip and white buttercream, pipe a bead border around the bottom of the cake.

Using the small round tip and brown buttercream, pipe a decorative border around the top of the cake then place reserved royal icing message on top of cake.

POPPY CUPCAKES

You Will Need:

Choose a cake flavor, see page 78-83, baked as cupcakes and cooled

Best Buttercream Frosting, see page 90 or Whipped Cream Frosting, see page 98

Gel or paste food coloring

Rapid tulip tip

Small leaf tip

Using the rapid tulip tip and yellow buttercream or whipped cream, pipe flowers on top of a cupcake.

Using the rapid tulip tip and white buttercream or whipped cream, pipe flowers on top of another cupcake.

Using the rapid tulip tip and orange buttercream or whipped cream, pipe flowers on top of another cupcake.

Using the small leaf tip and green buttercream, pipe leaves around the flowers as desired.

MOTHER'S DAY
##

Note: You will need to fill, stack and frost this cake before decorating (see page 8)

You Will Need:

Choose a cake flavor, see page 78-83, baked as two 7-inch layers and cooled

Choose one of the buttercream frostings, see page 90-92

Choose one of the fillings, see pages 100-102 (or use buttercream instead)

Gel or paste food colorings

Large round tip

Rapid starburst tip

Rapid poppy tip

Rapid tulip tip

Rose nail

Small rose tip

Small leaf tip

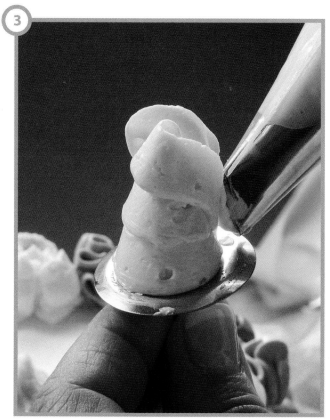

Using the large round tip and buttercream, pipe various green colored stems around the sides of the cake.

Using all three rapid tips and different color buttercream, squeeze flowers on top of the cake.

Using the small rose tip and buttercream, pipe a rose on top of the rose nail then place on top of the cake.

Make additional roses in different colors. See tips section on page 11 for how to pipe roses. Using the small leaf tip and green buttercream, add leaves between flowers as desired.

MASTER
CHOCOLATE CAKE

Note: Instead of baking cake layers from this recipe, you may start decorating more quickly by purchasing "naked" layers of un-iced cake from most bakeries.

Ingredients:

1 teaspoon kosher salt

1 teaspoon baking powder

2 teaspoons baking soda

3/4 cup cocoa powder

2 cups granulated sugar

1 3/4 cups all purpose flour

1 cup buttermilk

1 cup water

1/2 cup vegetable oil

2 large eggs

2 teaspoons vanilla extract

This Recipe Makes Enough For:

One 8-inch + one 4-inch layer

Two 7-inch layers

Three 6-inch layers

One 2-quart bowl-shaped cake

24 regular cupcakes

Method:

1. *Preheat oven to 350°F then apply baking spray to your chosen pan(s); set aside.*
2. *Sift salt, baking powder, baking soda, cocoa powder, sugar and flour into a large mixing bowl.*
3. *In a separate bowl whisk together remaining ingredients.*
4. *Pour the wet mixture into the dry ingredients then whisk until uniform.*
5. *Divide batter evenly between prepared pan(s).*
6. *Bake for 40-50 minutes or until a wooden pick inserted off-center comes out with just a few moist crumbs clinging to it.*
7. *Remove and let cool for 10 minutes then unmold onto a baking rack to cool.*
8. *Let cool completely before decorating.*

TIP

If you are pressed for time, you can use a store-bought chocolate cake mix and greatly improve it by substituting half & half for the water and melted butter for the oil. Keep the eggs the same. You can even use a sugar-free or gluten-free cake mix if desired.

MASTER
VANILLA CAKE

Note: Instead of baking cake layers from this recipe, you may start decorating more quickly by purchasing "naked" layers of un-iced cake from most bakeries.

Ingredients:

1 3/4 cups granulated sugar

1/2 cup unsalted butter, softened

1/2 cup solid white shortening

1 teaspoon kosher salt

1 tablespoon baking powder

1 teaspoon vanilla extract

1/8 teaspoon almond extract

5 large egg whites

2 3/4 cups cake flour

1 cup whole milk

This Recipe Makes Enough For:

One 8-inch + one 4-inch layer

Two 7-inch layers

Three 6-inch layers

One 2-quart bowl-shaped cake

24 regular cupcakes

Method:

1. *Preheat oven to 350°F and apply nonstick baking spray to your chosen pan(s); set aside.*
2. *Combine the sugar, butter, shortening, salt and baking powder in the bowl of a stand mixer fitted with the paddle attachment or use a stainless steel bowl and hand mixer.*
3. *Mix on medium speed for 5 minutes then scrape down the bowl.*
4. *Add the extracts and egg whites, mix well then scrape down bowl again.*
5. *Add remaining ingredients on low speed until just blended.*
6. *Divide batter evenly between the prepared pan(s).*
7. *Bake for 20-25 minutes or until a wooden pick inserted off-center comes out with just a few moist crumbs clinging to it.*
8. *Remove and let cool for 10 minutes then unmold onto a baking rack to cool.*
9. *Decorate when cold or frozen.*

TIP

If you are pressed for time, you can use a store-bought vanilla cake mix and greatly improve it by substituting half & half for the water and melted butter for the oil. Keep the eggs the same. You can even use a sugar-free or gluten-free cake mix if desired.

CAKES

RED VELVET CAKE

Note: Instead of baking cake layers from this recipe, you may start decorating more quickly by purchasing "naked" layers of un-iced cake from most bakeries.

Ingredients:

1/2 cup shortening

1 1/2 cups sugar

2 eggs

2 ounces red food coloring

2 tablespoons cocoa

1 teaspoon vanilla extract

2 1/4 cups all purpose flour, sifted

1 cup buttermilk

1 1/2 teaspoons kosher salt

1 tablespoon white vinegar

1 teaspoon baking soda

This Recipe Makes Enough For:

Two 9-inch fluted tart pans

One 8-inch + one 4-inch layer

Two 7-inch layers

Three 6-inch layers

One 2-quart bowl-shaped cake

24 regular cupcakes

CAKES

TIP

To make a Saint Patrick's Day cake, use green instead of red food coloring.

Method:

1. Preheat oven to 350°F and apply baking spray to your chosen pan(s): set aside.
2. Briefly cream together shortening and sugar using either a stand mixer fitted with the paddle attachment or a mixing bowl with a hand mixer.
3. Add eggs, mix on medium-high speed for 5 minutes then scrape down the sides of the bowl.
4. Mix for an additional 1 minute then add food coloring, cocoa and vanilla; mix until uniformly red in color.
5. Add flour and buttermilk alternately in 3 batches then scrape down the sides of the bowl.
6. Add salt, vinegar and baking soda then mix on high for 15 seconds.
7. Remove and divide batter evenly between the prepared pan(s).
8. Bake for 20-25 minutes or until a wooden pick inserted off-center comes out with just a few moist crumbs clinging to it.
9. Remove from oven then sprinkle 1 tablespoon of water evenly over each layer which helps to ensure cake is moist.
10. Let cool for 10 minutes then unmold onto a baking rack to cool.
11. Let cool then cover and refrigerate cake layers for up to two days before frosting and filling.

CHOCOLATE CHIP
COOKIE CAKE

Makes one 10-inch cake

Ingredients:

1 cup unsalted butter, softened

1 cup granulated sugar

1/2 cup light brown sugar, packed

2 cups all purpose flour

1 teaspoon baking soda

1 teaspoon kosher salt

2 teaspoons vanilla extract

2 large eggs

2 cups assorted chocolate chips and chunks

TIP

To make different cookie cakes, try using nuts, crushed pretzels, caramel bits or butterscotch chips. Also, for a lazy day you can use two tubs of store-bought dough instead of making it from scratch and just follow the baking instructions in the recipe.

Method:

1. *Preheat oven to 325°F and apply baking spray to a 10-inch cake pan; set aside.*
2. *Place the butter and both sugars into a large mixing bowl then cream together using a hand mixer on medium speed.*
3. *Add remaining ingredients in the order listed then mix until just combined.*
4. *Scrape dough into prepared pan then pat into an even layer, trying not to disturb the baking spray.*
5. *Bake for 30 minutes or until the top is dry and a knife inserted in the center comes out clean.*
6. *Remove and let cool completely before unmolding and decorating.*

BROWNIE
CAKE

Makes one 9x9-inch square cake

Ingredients:

1 cup (2 sticks) unsalted butter, softened

2 cups granulated sugar

4 large eggs

1/4 teaspoon kosher salt

1 teaspoon vanilla extract

1/2 cup good quality cocoa

1 cup unbleached all purpose flour (can be gluten-free)

1/2 cup mixed nuts (optional)

1/2 cup chocolate chips (optional)

Method:

1. *Preheat oven to 350°F then apply nonstick baking spray to a 9x9-inch pan and set aside.*
2. *Using a hand mixer and mixing bowl, beat the butter until fluffy.*
3. *Add the sugar and eggs then mix to combine.*
4. *Add remaining ingredients, mix just until combined then scrape into prepared pan.*
5. *Bake for 1 hour or until a wooden pick inserted off-center emerges clean.*
6. *Remove and let cool completely before decorating.*

TIP

Baking nonstick spray is a modern day miracle for keeping baked goods from sticking to the pan. This is the best way to ensure that your creations come out of the pan easily and completely intact.

LEMON
CHEESECAKE

Makes one 8-inch cake

Note: Instead of baking the cheesecake from this recipe, you may start decorating more quickly by purchasing a plain topped cheesecake from most bakeries.

Ingredients:

12 store-bought shortbread cookies, crumbled into fine crumbs

2 pounds (four 8-ounce packages) cream cheese, softened

1 cup granulated sugar

5 large eggs

Zest and juice of 2 lemons

Method:

1. *Place a large pan or skillet with 1-inch of water in the oven then preheat to 300°F.*
2. *Wrap the exterior of an 8-inch springform pan with aluminum foil then apply a heavy layer of baking spray to the interior of the pan.*
3. *Scatter shortbread crumbs over the bottom of the pan in an even layer; set aside.*
4. *Combine remaining ingredients in a blender, food processor or mixer until smooth.*
5. *Into the springform pan with cookie crumbs at the bottom, pour the cream cheese mixture then carefully place inside the large pan or skillet with water in the oven.*
6. *Bake for 90 minutes, rotating pan halfway through baking, or until just set. To test for doneness, cake should jiggle when tapped but not ripple and internal temperature should be 155°F on a thermometer.*
7. *Remove from oven, let cool for 1 hour then wrap and chill for a minimum of 24 hours or up to 5 days.*
8. *Do not attempt to decorate cake until completely cold.*

TO MAKE PUMPKIN CHEESECAKE

Omit lemon zest and juice then add 1/4 cup canned pumpkin puree, 1 tablespoon pumpkin pie spice, 1 teaspoon ground cinnamon, 1/4 teaspoon ground nutmeg and 2 teaspoons vanilla extract to the blender, food processor or mixer in step 4.

BEST BUTTERCREAM
FROSTING

Makes 5 cups

Note: Instead of making the buttercream from this recipe, you may start decorating more quickly by purchasing buttercream sold in tubs from many bakeries or craft stores.

Ingredients:

2/3 cup egg whites (about 6 large egg whites) these must not contain any yolk

1 1/3 cups granulated sugar

1/2 teaspoon kosher salt

2 teaspoons clear imitation vanilla

1 pound (4 sticks) unsalted butter, cool, not cold or warm, sliced very thinly

Method:

1. *Fashion a double boiler using a clean mixing bowl nested in a stockpot holding 1-inch of simmering water.*

2. *Place egg whites and sugar into the bowl then whisk using a clean whisk until uniform in color.*

3. *Continue whisking slowly for an additional 5-6 minutes or until hot to the touch (only touch with clean fingers) and no grains of sugar remain. At this point the mixture should be 160°F.*

4. *Remove and use a hand mixer with beaters or stand mixer with whisk attachment to beat egg mixture for 5 minutes or until semi-stiff peaks form then beat in the salt and vanilla.*

5. *Add the butter, a few slices at a time, until incorporated (about 1 minute to add all the butter) then beat until mixture is thick and uniform in texture and any signs of graininess or curdling are gone and mixture is smooth.*

6. *Frosting is now ready to use.*

7. *Any unused buttercream can be kept refrigerated in a sealed container for up to 2 weeks or frozen for up to 3 months.*

8. *Bring to room temperature and beat again before using.*

FROSTING

If you are using store-bought buttercream and it is too stiff or soft, you can use a hand mixer to beat in cool butter and it will become fluffy enough to pipe well.

You will not be able to achieve semi-stiff peaks in step 4 if any fat or egg yolks get into the egg whites in the beginning of this recipe. For that reason, it is extremely important to keep everything clean and fat free. Egg yolks contain fat so if you are worried about separating eggs properly, you can purchase the pasteurized egg whites from a carton which is available in the dairy section of your grocery store.

If you want your buttercream to look really white rather than off-white, you can add some white food coloring.

EASY BUTTERCREAM
FROSTING

Makes 3 cups

Ingredients:

1 pound (4 sticks) unsalted butter

1 can (16 ounces) store-bought frosting, can be sugar-free, without chips or sprinkles

Method:

1. *Using a hand mixer or a stand mixer with either paddle or beater attachment, cream butter until smooth and fluffy.*
2. *Add the frosting then mix until smooth and uniform in color.*

TIP

If it is very hot in your kitchen, you can use half butter and half shortening to achieve a firmer buttercream that is less prone to melting.

CHOCOLATE GANACHE
FROSTING

Makes 1 2/3 cups

Ingredients:

8 ounces (1 cup) heavy cream

12 ounces (1 1/2 cups) semi-sweet chocolate chips (good quality)

Method:

1. *Pour heavy cream into a microwave-safe bowl then heat until very hot.*
2. *Add the chocolate chips to the bowl and let stand for 1 minute.*
3. *Whisk gently until completely smooth.*
4. *Use right away if you want to use it as a glaze.*
5. *Let cool until mixture thickens if you want to use it as frosting.*
6. *Chill slightly if you want to pipe it.*
7. *Ganache will keep in the refrigerator for up to 2 weeks.*

TIP

For white chocolate ganache, decrease cream to 2/3 cup and use 12 ounces white chocolate chips. For silky and shiny ganache, it is important to use high quality chocolate. Do not try to make this recipe using candy coating type "chocolates," as the ganache will have a "grainy" texture.

MERINGUE
FROSTING

Makes 4 cups

Ingredients:

1 cup egg whites from freshly cracked eggs (not from a store-bought carton)

2 cups granulated sugar

1/8 teaspoon vanilla bean seeds (optional)

Method:

1. *It is important to keep everything grease-free.*

2. *Heat 1-inch of water in a saucepot over medium-high heat then rest the clean bowl of your stand mixer or a stainless steel bowl on the rim of the saucepot to make a double boiler.*

3. *Whisk egg whites and sugar in the stand mixer bowl or a stainless steel bowl over the double boiler until quite warm to the touch (make sure hands are very clean) and sugar has dissolved. To test, pinch some mixture between thumb and finger until you do not feel any sugar grains. If you still feel sugar grains, heat for an additional minute or until completely smooth and temperature reaches 160°F on a thermometer.*

4. *Transfer stand mixer bowl to a stand mixer then attach clean whisk attachment. If using the stainless bowl, remove from saucepot then use clean beaters with a hand mixer.*

5. *Whip on high speed until stiff peaks form then add vanilla bean seeds if using.*

6. *When finished, use mixture within 8-10 minutes before it starts to lose its body and shine. If you want it to look like the photo, use the zig zag ball tip then brown using a blow torch.*

FROSTING

TIP

The higher proportion of sugar and the heat from the double boiler gives this meringue incredible stability. It is completely different, more beautiful and more versatile than the usual American meringue. You can also toast the piped meringue using a blow torch or broil until brown. If using vanilla bean seeds, make sure they are not from a jar that contains glycerine or any oil-based ingredient or the meringue will deflate as soon as you add it and become too liquid to pipe.

MIRROR GLAZE

Note: Only use this recipe as a glaze, do not use for piping

Ingredients:

For the Glaze (makes 3 cups, enough to cover a 10-inch cake)

A smooth, frozen cake, for glazing

1/2 cup cold water

5 teaspoons unflavored, plain gelatin

1 cup granulated sugar

1/4 cup additional water

1/2 cup light corn syrup

1/2 cup sweetened condensed milk

8 ounces white chocolate chips

Food colorings of your choice + white food coloring

For Decorating

Choose one of the buttercream frostings, see page 90-92

Rapid tulip tip

Small leaf tip

Method:

1. *Ensure your cake is frozen, smooth, free of loose crumbs and set on a sheet pan fitted with a cake rack. Keep in freezer until ready to glaze.*

2. *In a small microwave-safe bowl, quickly whisk 1/2 cup water and gelatin together; set aside.*

3. *In a separate microwave-safe bowl, combine the sugar and additional 1/4 cup water; microwave until boiling then remove.*

4. *Microwave the gelatin mixture for 40 seconds or until steamy and clear.*

5. *Pour gelatin mixture into the hot sugar mixture and stir gently using a spoon (do not use a whisk as it will create air bubbles and ruin the smooth look of the poured glaze).*

6. *Add the corn syrup, condensed milk and chocolate then let rest for 2 minutes to allow chocolate to melt. Stir again slowly using a spoon until melted.*

7. *Strain mixture to remove any lumps.*

8. *Cover bowl with plastic wrap and let cool to approximately 90°F which is the optimal pouring temperature that achieves a nice thickness of shiny glaze when poured.*

9. *Mix about 1 teaspoon of white food coloring into the glaze to whiten then divide mixture into three smaller bowls. Leave one bowl white, then color one pink and one red.*

10. *Gently pour the red and pink glaze into the white glaze without stirring.*

11. *Remove sheet pan with cake from freezer, keeping cake on the rack.*

12. *Pour glaze over the cake until completely covered with glaze.*

13. *Let stand for 5 minutes to solidify then trim excess mixture away from the base of the cake using a small knife.*

14. *Transfer cake to a serving plate then add a row of flowers around the cake using buttercream and the rapid tulip tip. Finish by adding leaves using the small leaf tip and green buttercream.*

TIP

You can be creative and make this glaze using any colors you want. No cake ever turns out exactly the same as they are all uniquely beautiful. Excess mixture can be scraped up, warmed and used again although the colors will usually become somewhat "muddy".

WHIPPED CREAM
FROSTING

Makes 3 cups

Ingredients:

2 cups heavy cream, very cold

1/4 cup granulated sugar or other sweetener

1/2 teaspoon vanilla extract

Method:

1. *In a large mixing bowl using a hand mixer, balloon whisk or immersion blender, whisk all ingredients on medium speed until stiff peaks form but mixture is still very smooth.*

2. *Use mixture within 20 minutes while still cold or it starts to separate and won't pipe nicely. Once it's piped it will stay nice for 12 hours if kept cold.*

TIP

To color whipped cream, stir in a few drops of either gel or paste type of food coloring. Whipped cream absorbs food coloring differently than buttercream so you may need to add a bit more color than usual to achieve the color depth you desire.

ROYAL ICING

Makes 1 1/2 cups

Ingredients:

3 ounces egg whites, can be from a store-bought carton

1/4 teaspoon cream of tartar

4 cups powdered sugar

Method:

1. *Combine all ingredients in the bowl of a stand mixer fitted with the whisk attachment or use a stainless steel mixing bowl and a hand mixer with the beaters.*

2. *Mix on low speed until blended then whip on high speed for 6 minutes or until stiff peaks form.*

3. *Use as desired, keeping the bowl covered at all times as mixture will crust easily.*

TIP

When piping messages with royal icing, make them well ahead of time so that they have time to harden. Let rest uncovered for a minimum of 24 hours at room temperature. Also remember to pipe extras as they are fragile.

LEMON CURD
FILLING

Makes 2 1/2 cups

Ingredients:

3 large egg yolks

2 large eggs

Zest from 2 lemons

1/3 cup fresh lemon juice

1/2 cup granulated sugar

2 sticks cold butter, diced

1/4 teaspoon dry turmeric (optional for color)

Method:

1. *Place all ingredients into a high-powered blender; cover with lid.*
2. *Blend for 4 minutes on the highest speed.*
3. *Stop blender then use a thermometer to check if temperature has reached 180°F. If necessary, continue blending in 1-minute intervals until 180°F is reached.*
4. *Remove, let cool for 20 minutes then pour into a storage jar or container and refrigerate.*
5. *Curd will keep in the refrigerator for up to one week or in the freezer for up to 3 months.*
6. *Stir before using.*

TIP

This recipe can also be made on the stove top using a double boiler. Whisk slowly over simmering water for 5-8 minutes or until thickened.

PASTRY CREAM
FILLING

Makes 2 1/2 cups

Ingredients:

1/2 cup sugar

1/4 cup cornstarch

A pinch of kosher salt

4 large egg yolks

2 cups half & half

1 vanilla bean, split or 1 teaspoon pure vanilla extract

Method:

1. *With the stovetop turned off, whisk together the sugar, cornstarch, salt and egg yolks in a medium saucepan.*

2. *In a microwave-safe bowl, combine the half & half and vanilla bean then microwave until very hot.*

3. *While whisking the saucepan mixture fast, pour in the hot half & half mixture slowly while continuing to whisk fast until combined.*

4. *Turn on the stovetop to medium heat and whisk steadily using a whisk or rubber spatula until mixture comes to a full boil. Stir and scrape all over the pan bottom to prevent sticking and scorching.*

5. *Remove saucepan from heat then remove vanilla bean if using and wash it off, dry and save vanilla bean for another use.*

6. *Transfer cream to a container and press a piece of plastic wrap directly on the surface to prevent a skin from forming.*

7. *Chill and use to fill any of the cakes you choose to make.*

STRAWBERRY FILLING

Makes 2 cups

Ingredients:

3 cups fresh strawberries, chopped

1/3 cup granulated sugar

2 tablespoons fresh lemon juice

4 tablespoons pectin powder

Method:

1. *In a mixing bowl gently toss together strawberries, sugar and lemon.*
2. *Let rest for 10 minutes.*
3. *Thoroughly stir in the pectin and let rest for an additional 10 minutes or until thickened.*
4. *Use as a filling or as desired.*

PESTO DIP

Makes 1 1/2 cups

Ingredients:

1 package (8 ounces) cream cheese, softened

1/3 cup jarred pesto

1/3 cup Parmesan cheese, grated

Method:

1. *Whisk all ingredients together in a mixing bowl until smooth.*
2. *Fit piping bag with coupler and small star tip then fill with pesto mixture.*
3. *Pipe as desired and serve.*

TIP

To make a curry-flavored dip, omit the pesto and add 1 tablespoon curry powder, 1 teaspoon minced ginger, 1 teaspoon minced garlic and 1 teaspoon red Fresno or jalapeño chiles. To make a sun dried tomato dip, omit the pesto and add 1/3 cup finely minced sun dried tomatoes.

DEVILED EGGS

Makes 10 servings

Ingredients:

10 large eggs

1/2 cup mayonnaise

2 teaspoons yellow mustard

2 tablespoons sweet pickle relish

1/2 teaspoon granulated sugar

A pinch of cayenne pepper

1 teaspoon kosher salt

2 teaspoons cider vinegar

Paprika for sprinkling (optional)

Method:

1. *Place eggs into a large stockpot then add cold water until eggs are covered by 1-inch cold water.*

2. *Bring to a boil over high heat.*

3. *As soon as water starts to boil, set a timer for 10 minutes then reduce heat to low.*

4. *When time is up, remove stockpot from heat then add cold water.*

5. *As soon as eggs have cooled enough to handle (still hot), crack each one all over to allow some water to get between the shell and the eggs.*

6. *Peel each egg under a fairly hard flow of cold water from the faucet.*

7. *Not all of the eggs will be perfect, you want more yolks anyway so it's fine.*

8. *Let peeled eggs stand in cold water for 10 minutes or until completely cool.*

9. *Cut eggs in half, saving all of the yolks then find another use for any torn egg whites.*

10. *Combine yolks, mayonnaise, mustard, relish, sugar, cayenne pepper, salt and vinegar in a food processor until smooth.*

11. *Fit piping bag with coupler and small rose tip then fill with egg mixture; refrigerate until ready to use.*

12. *Rinse egg whites, place on a serving platter then pipe with filling.*

13. *Cover and refrigerate until ready to serve.*

TIP

To stop the eggs from rolling around on the serving platter, scatter some thinly shaved lettuce on the platter first. The filling can be changed easily by adding crumbled bacon or blue cheese.

GARLIC HERB
SPREAD

Makes 1 1/2 cups

Ingredients:

1 package (8 ounces) cream cheese, softened

1/4 cup (1/2 stick) unsalted butter, softened

1/4 cup mayonnaise

Sriracha hot sauce to taste

Kosher salt and fresh pepper to taste

2 garlic cloves, finely chopped

3 green onions, finely minced

1 teaspoon fresh oregano, finely chopped

1 teaspoon store-bought anchovy paste from a tube (optional)

Method:

1. *In a small mixing bowl, whisk together all ingredients until smooth.*
2. *Fit piping bag with coupler and large star tip then fill with mixture.*
3. *Pipe as desired and serve.*

CREAM CHEESE
MINTS

Makes 6 dozen

Ingredients:

3 ounces cream cheese, softened

2 tablespoons unsalted butter, softened

3 cups powdered sugar, sifted

A few drops peppermint oil or extract or to taste

A few drops food coloring of your choice

Method:

1. *Thoroughly combine all ingredients in a mixing bowl until smooth.*
2. *Fit piping bag with coupler and desired tip then fill with mixture.*
3. *Using the small rose tip, large round tip, rapid starburst tip and small star tip, pipe mixture into desired small shapes such as hearts, rosettes and dots onto bare cookie sheets.*
4. *Let dry at room temperature for 1-2 days or until dry.*
5. *Gently loosen mints using a spatula and flip over then let dry for an additional day.*
6. *Store in an airtight container at room temperature for up to 2 months.*

TWICE BAKED
POTATOES

Makes 12 potatoes

Ingredients:

24 small Red Bliss or Yukon Gold potatoes

3 tablespoons unsalted butter, melted + more for drizzling

3 tablespoons cream cheese, melted

3 tablespoons heavy cream + more as needed

Kosher salt and fresh pepper to taste

1/4 cup Cheddar cheese, grated

Fresh chives, for serving

Method:

1. *Boil potatoes in salted simmering water for 20 minutes or until tender when pierced with the tip of a paring knife then drain and let cool for 10 minutes.*
2. *Cut off top 1/3 of each potato then use a kitchen towel and a small spoon to remove most of the potato from the skins, leaving just enough for skins to hold their shape.*
3. *Place 12 of the best looking empty skins on a sheet pan then discard remaining skins.*
4. *In a mixing bowl, mash together the insides of the potatoes with remaining ingredients, except Cheddar cheese and chives, until smooth.*
5. *Add more cream if mixture is too thick.*
6. *Fit piping bag with coupler and rapid starburst tip then fill with mixture.*
7. *Season empty potato skins with salt and pepper then pipe potato filling onto skins.*
8. *Drizzle tops with additional melted butter, season with salt and pepper then top with Cheddar cheese.*
9. *Broil potatoes in the oven for 3-5 minutes or until hot and edges are browned.*
10. *Remove, top with chives and serve hot.*

TIP
This recipe also looks really nice when made with fingerling potatoes.

ANTS ON A

LOG

Makes 4 servings

Ingredients:

8 celery stalks

Dark raisins as needed

1 cup regular creamy peanut butter

Method:

1. *Trim celery into desired lengths.*
2. *Place celery on a serving platter.*
3. *Fit piping bag with coupler and small star tip then fill with peanut butter.*
4. *Pipe peanut butter down the lengths of the celery using small, circular motions.*
5. *Arrange raisins ("ants") on top of peanut butter as desired before serving.*

TIP

This recipe is best made using the regular kind of creamy peanut butter. Natural peanut butter is too runny to hold shape when piped and the chunky kind will not pass through the star tip nicely. If you are allergic to nuts, use softened cream cheese instead of nut butters.

SALMON
CREAM CHEESE

Makes 2 1/2 cups

Ingredients:

2 packages (8 ounces each) cream cheese, softened

1/4 cup mayonnaise

1 tablespoon fresh lemon juice

1 tablespoon capers, drained

Kosher salt and fresh pepper to taste

1/2 cup smoked salmon + more for garnish

1 teaspoon fresh dill + more for garnishing

Yellow and red food coloring (optional)

Sliced cucumber, for serving (optional)

Method:

1. *Combine all ingredients, except food coloring, in a food processor until smooth.*
2. *If the color is pale, add 3 drops yellow food coloring and 1 drop red if desired.*
3. *Fit piping bag with coupler and small star tip then fill with salmon mixture.*
4. *Pipe as desired.*

SOURCE PAGE

Here are some of my favorite places to find ingredients that are not readily available at grocery stores as well as kitchen tools and supplies that help you become a better cook.

The Bakers Catalogue at King Arthur Flour

Gel or paste food colorings, piping bags, baking pans and cake pans, blow torches, rubber and silicone spatulas, digital timers, meringue powder, oven thermometers, candy thermometers, the best instant read thermometers, off-set spatulas, measuring cups and spoons, knives, cookie sheets, jimmies, colored sugar and sprinkles
www.kingarthurflour.com

Wilton Enterprises

Everything needed for cake decorating. Cake decorating turntables, cake pans, spatulas, cake icer tips, colored sugars, sprinkles, gel and paste food coloring, edible gold luster dust, sprinkles, fondant, gum paste, royal icing mix, meringue powder, cake scrapers and side smoothers, decorating tips, piping bags and couplers. Wilton also sells many of their supplies at Michael's crafts, Jo-Ann crafts and Walmart.
www.wilton.com

Etsy

Unique and specialty cupcake liners
www.etsy.com

Nui Enterprises

My favorite pure vanilla extract and the best quality vanilla beans
www.vanillafromtahiti.com

Whole Foods

Natural food coloring, natural and organic baking ingredients, natural parchment paper, good quality chocolate such as Valhrona and Callebaut
www.wholefoods.com

Kerekes the Chef Station

All varieties of cake pans, edible gold luster dust, spatulas, cake decorating turntables, cake scrapers and cake side smoothers
www.bakedeco.com

Chocosphere

Excellent quality cocoa (Callebaut) All Chocolates, Jimmies and sprinkles
www.chocosphere.com

INDEX